SIMPLE MACHINES

LEVERS ARE MACHINES

DOUGLAS BENDER

A Crabtree Roots Plus Book

CRABTREE
Publishing Company
www.crabtreebooks.com

School-to-Home Support for Caregivers and Teachers

This book helps children grow by letting them practice reading. Here are a few guiding questions to help the reader with building his or her comprehension skills. Possible answers appear here in red.

Before Reading:

- What do I think this book is about?
    - *I think this book is about a simple machine called a lever.*
    - *I think this book is about the levers we use every day.*
- What do I want to learn about this topic?
    - *I want to learn the different levers in my world.*
    - *I want to learn more about simple machines.*

During Reading:

- I wonder why...
    - *I wonder why levers can be big or small.*
    - *I wonder why some simple machines have no moving parts.*
- What have I learned so far?
    - *I have learned that the tab on a can of soda is a small lever.*
    - *I have learned that a seesaw is a big lever.*

After Reading:

- What details did I learn about this topic?
    - *I have learned that a fishing rod is a type of lever.*
    - *I have learned that my arm can be used as a lever.*
- Read the book again and look for the vocabulary words.
    - *I see the word* ***fulcrum*** *on page 9 and the words* ***fishing rod*** *on page 18. The other vocabulary words are found on page 23.*

This is a **lever**.

Pulley **Lever**

Screw

A lever is a **simple machine**. There are six simple machines.

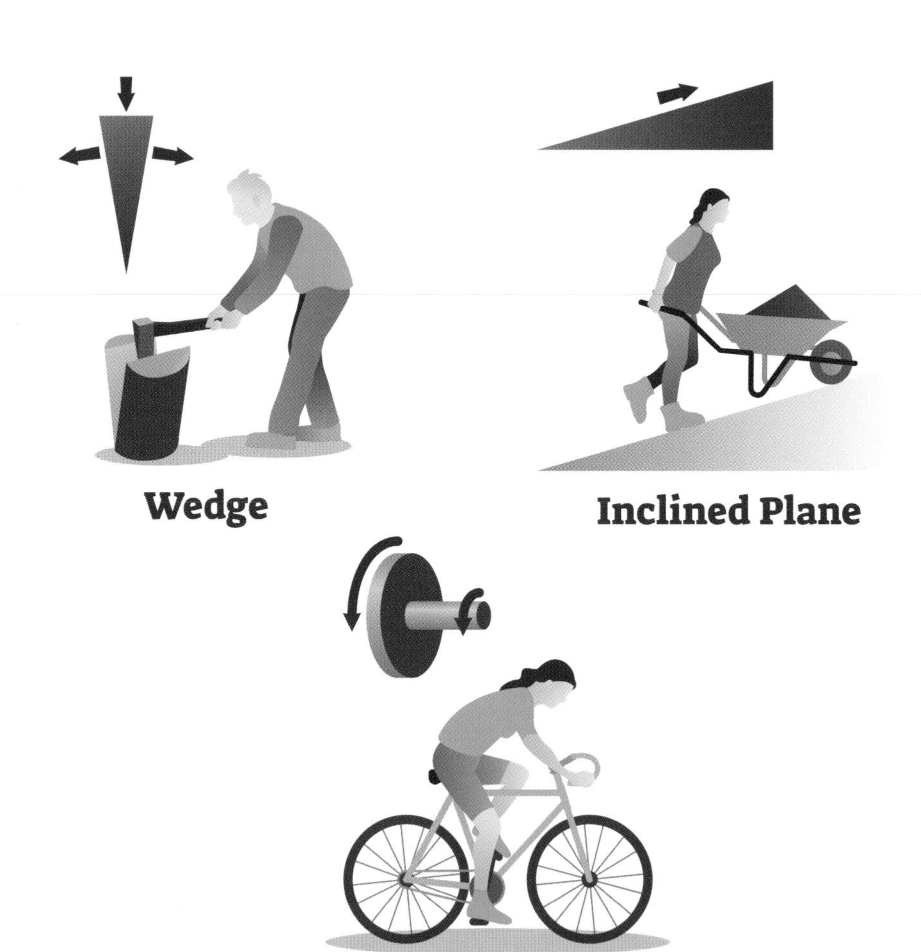

Simple machines have few or no moving parts.

Levers help us move things more easily.

A lever uses a long or short **bar**.

It turns on a **fulcrum**.

When we push down on one end of the bar, the **load** lifts on the other end.

bar
fulcrum
load

Some levers are big.

Some levers are small.

The tab on a can of pop is a small lever.

A **seesaw** is a big lever.

Sarah and Tom
move up and down
on the seesaw!

A **fishing rod** is also a lever.

Even your arm
can be a lever!

Word List

Sight Words

a
also
are
arm
be
big
can
down
even
few
help
is
long
move
no
of
on
one
or
other
parts
pop
short
small
some
tab
the
this
turns
up
us
uses
your

Words to Know

bar

fishing rod

fulcrum

lever

load

seesaw

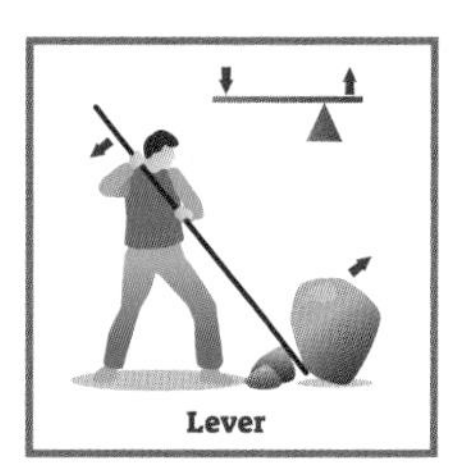

simple machine

Written by: Douglas Bender
Designed by: Rhea Wallace
Series Development: James Earley
Proofreader: Janine Deschenes
Production coordinator
and Prepress technician: Katherine Berti
Print coordinator: Katherine Berti
Educational Consultant: Marie Lemke M.Ed.

Photographs:
Shutterstock: logoboom: cover, pg 1; JN999: p. 3, 23; Granpa: p. 7; Tetiana Cherkasgyna: p. 8, 9, 23; Rozhov Denis: p. 11; Olga Rolenko: p. 12; richard johnson: p. 13; Somchai Son: p. 15; PSD Photography: p. 16-17; Redpixel: p. 18, 23; Rusamee: p. 21

SIMPLE MACHINES

LEVERS ARE MACHINES

Library and Archives Canada Cataloguing in Publication

CIP available at Library and Archives Canada

Library of Congress Cataloging-in-Publication Data

CIP available at Library of Congress

Crabtree Publishing Company

www.crabtreebooks.com 1-800-387-7650

Printed in the U.S.A./CG20210915/012022

Copyright © 2022 **CRABTREE PUBLISHING COMPANY**

All rights reserved. No part of this publication may be reproduced, stored in a retrieval system or be transmitted in any form or by any means, electronic, mechanical, photocopying, recording, or otherwise, without the prior written permission of Crabtree Publishing Company.
In Canada: We acknowledge the financial support of the Government of Canada through the Canada Book Fund for our publishing activities.

Published in the United States
Crabtree Publishing
347 Fifth Avenue, Suite 1402-145
New York, NY, 10016

Published in Canada
Crabtree Publishing
616 Welland Ave.
St. Catharines, ON, L2M 5V6